DUDLEY COLL
TEL. O138
Books are to be returned on or t
Books may be renewed by telep
subject to conditions.

C000075906

Developing literacy skills: supporting achievement

126978

NIACE lifelines in adult learning

The *NIACE lifelines in adult learning* series provides straightforward background and information, accessible know-how and useful examples of good practice for all practitioners involved in adult and community learning. Focusing in turn on different areas of adult learning these guides are an essential part of every practitioner's toolkit.

1. Community education and neighbourhood renewal – Jane Thompson, ISBN 1 86201 139 7
2. Spreading the word: reaching out to new learners – Veronica McGivney, ISBN 1 86201 140 0
3. Managing community projects for change – Jan Eldred, ISBN 1 86201 141 9
4. Engaging black learners in adult and community education – Lenford White, ISBN 1 86201 142 7
5. Consulting adults – Chris Jude, ISBN 1 86201 194 4
6. Working with young adults – Carol Jackson, ISBN 1 86201 150 8
7. Promoting learning – Kate Malone, ISBN 1 86201 151 6
8. Evaluating community projects – Jane Field, ISBN 1 86201 152 4
9. Working in partnership – Lyn Tett, ISBN 1 86201 162 1
10. Working with Asian heritage communities – David McNulty, ISBN 1 86201 174 5
11. Learning and community arts – Tony Fegan, ISBN 1 86201 181 8
12. Museums and community learning – Garrick Fincham, ISBN 1 86201 182 6
13. Developing a needs-based library service – John Pateman, ISBN 1 86201 183 4
14. Volunteers and volunteering – Janet Swinney, ISBN 1 86201 187 7
15. Sustaining projects for success – Kay Snowdon, ISBN 1 86201 188 5
16. Opening up schools for adults – Judith Summers, ISBN 1 86201 192 3
17. Befriending learners – Jane Field, ISBN 1 86201 210 5
18. Developing literacy: supporting achievement – Amanda Lindsay and Judith Gawn, ISBN 1 86201 216 4
19. Developing numeracy: supporting achievement – Barbara Newmarch, ISBN 1 86201 217 2
20. Developing ESOL: supporting achievement – Violet Windsor and Christina Healey, ISBN 1 86201 218 0
21. Developing embedded literacy, language and numeracy: supporting achievement – Jan Eldred, ISBN 1 86201 219 9
   The Jargon Buster – Yanina Dutton, ISBN 1 86201 215 6

niace · lifelines in adult learning

18

DUDLEY COLLEGE LIBRARY

Developing literacy skills: supporting achievement

Amanda Lindsay
and Judith Gawn

126978 ✓
BWL 374.0124 LIN
dup

Published by the National Institute of
Adult Continuing Education (England and Wales)

21 De Montfort Street
Leicester LE1 7GE
Company registration no. 2603322
Charity registration no. 1002775

First published 2005

© 2005 National Institute of Adult Continuing Education (England and Wales)

All rights reserved. No reproduction, copy or transmission of this publication
may be made without the written permission of the publishers, save in
accordance with the provisions of the Copyright, Designs and Patents Act 1988,
or under the terms of any licence permitting limited copying issue by the
Copyright Licensing Agency.

The *NIACE lifelines in adult learning series* is supported by the Adult
and Community Learning Fund. ACLF is funded by the Department
for Education and Skills and managed in partnership by NIACE and
the Basic Skills Agency to develop widening participation in adult learning.

promoting adult learning

NIACE has a broad remit to promote lifelong learning
opportunities for adults. NIACE works to develop
increased participation in education and training,
particularly for those who do not have easy access
because of barriers of class, gender, age, race,
language and culture, learning difficulties and
disabilities, or insufficient financial resources.

www.niace.org.uk

Cataloguing in Publication Data
A CIP record of this title is available from the British Library

Designed and typeset by Boldface
Printed in Great Britain by Russell Press, Nottingham
All photographs © Sue Parkins, NIACE

ISBN 1 86201 216 4

Contents

Note to the reader

Inspirations: refer to case studies and examples of good practice.

Introduction

This book is for practitioners who are developing their skills and understanding as teachers of literacy in adult education, or as teaching assistants or volunteers. It is not a substitute for training but it should provide you with an insight into the contexts in which adult literacy takes place and the subject knowledge required of teachers. It should also provide you with an understanding of good practice and where to go for further information. The guide may also be useful for those who have responsibility for planning and developing literacy provision.

The Government's *Skills for Life* strategy, aimed at reducing the numbers of adults with 'poor' literacy, numeracy and language skills was launched in 2001.

The thrust of the strategy in the first two years was on building capacity, both of teachers and the contexts in which adult literacy, numeracy and language was being delivered. The focus now is very much on raising the quality of provision and with that comes additional requirements on organisations within the field around processes and systems that should be put in place to ensure this happens. Much of what is required is good practice, in terms of teaching and learning, but for organisations working with learners who have been disengaged from formal learning, there are some additional challenges.

Ultimately our work must be about ensuring that learners do indeed participate in a positive, life-enhancing learning experience. The processes and systems that you implement should meet quality audits and inspection requirements, but they must also be appropriate for the contexts in which you are working, be relevant to the needs and lives of your learners and be part of a shared dialogue between managers, teachers and learners.

1 Adult literacy learners

Who needs adult literacy?

The government has estimated that 7 million people in the UK have a reading and writing ability below level 2 – by their definition the level that should be reached by an 11 year old. It has invested £1.6 billion from April 2003 – March 2006 with the target of helping 1.5 million adults improve their skills by 2007.

Skills for Life priority groups include unemployed people, prisoners and adults on probation, low-skilled employees and other people at risk of social exclusion, such as refugees and asylum seekers, the homeless and travelling families. The strategy has also targeted parents through programmes such as Step in to Learning, Link Up and Skills for Families.

Of course very many of these adults are in work, competently holding down jobs, bringing up families and participating in all of the activities that many of us involve ourselves in. Many adults would like to improve their reading and writing skills in order to seek promotion, to find a new job, to help their children with schoolwork or simply to reduce worry and anxiety.

> "I kept it hidden until I was about 17 and I went to work at this warehouse... I went for the first day and they gave me sheets of paper and they said, 'You won't be getting any orders out on the first day, but after the first week we expect you to start doing orders'. They're showing me these orders and they might have just scribbled on the paper, I couldn't have understood them any better... I went in to the boss and told him I was quitting the job. They wanted an explanation why I was leaving and I got forced into a corner there, so I just told them.
>
> They said, 'Well, maybe we can overcome this.' So they got a list of paper and went round the shop with me and just wrote odd things out on the slip. 'Can you read them?' So I said, 'Well I'll try anything once.'
>
> Amazingly, out of ten things he wrote down, I think I got six of them right. So things went on from there. I didn't give my job up."
> *Writings about Workplace Learning,* Lancaster University, 1992

However, many learners will have had limited or negative experiences of school education and few will have recognised qualifications. Most learners will probably have grown up in the UK while others, particularly in inner-city areas, may have grown up in other English speaking places, such as the Caribbean.

Increasing numbers of speakers of other languages are fluent enough in spoken English to participate actively in a literacy classroom. This may be because they have grown up in a country where English is the 'official' language, such as Nigeria, or they may have learnt English in this country. Despite the fact that these learners want to work on their written English and reading, they may have high-level qualifications from their countries of origin and a literacy course is not always the best place to meet their needs.

Learners in one adult literacy classroom may be a homogenous group of people from a small tight-knit community, in another they may be from different corners of the globe with vastly different educational and life experiences, with

"When I was at school in Jamaica we used to use a slate to write on. As Jamaica was a British colony the slate was sent over from Wales. It was very cheap to buy, cheaper than exercise book. You couldn't tear it and it lasted much longer. You could still use the slate even if it broke... I didn't like going to school much. The rough kids would hit me on the head with the slate and take my pocket money – just like the kids here!

When people couldn't go to school they cried because they had lots of work to do at home. At school there was more playing, not like today."
Write On Deptford: Deptford Bookshop and Literacy Centre, 1997

ages ranging from 17 to 80+ and with a wide variety of needs and aims. A literacy teacher today has to be equipped to meet the challenges and the demands of these different groups.

Different contexts for literacy learning

Adult literacy is now offered in FE colleges, local authority-funded community courses, libraries the voluntary and community sector, in prisons, the probation service, through Jobcentre Plus, Learndirect, the workplace and within family learning programmes.

Some of this provision is free-standing, some is embedded in vocational courses and other activities. These different contexts and situations require different approaches and practices that address the particular needs and purposes of the learners. For example, a literacy course in a small community organisation may focus on creative writing and reading for pleasure, whereas learning taking place in a car factory may focus on health and safety issues, trade union rights and essential reading for work.

Examples of good practice in different contexts
Go to the Literacy Trust website for some excellent examples of good practice in literacy and numeracy in a range of contexts with adults in the community: museums and libraries, a café, churches, housing association, probation service and other community projects. The website provides evaluations of the projects and links to each of them.
www.literacytrust.org.uk/socialinclusion/adults/goodpractice

Raising Standards: DfES Contextual Guides
The DfES had produced 10 guides to raise standards and support success in literacy, numeracy and ESOL provision. They are designed to help practitioners and managers interpret the Common Inspection Framework for the particular circumstances of their work. Each guide addresses a specific context:
- Adult and community learning
- E-learning
- Embedded learning
- Family learning
- Further education colleges
- Jobcentre Plus programmes
- Learners with learning difficulties and/or disabilities
- Prisons
- Work-based learning
- Young Offender Institutions for Young People Aged 18-21

Copies of all of these guides are available free from: DfES Publicataions, PO Box 5050, Annesley, Nottingham NG15 0DJ, Tel 0845 602 2260 or E-mail: dfes@prolog.uk.com

2 Encouraging participation

Linked to the *Skills for Life* strategy is the Learning and Skills Council (LSC)'s Widening Adult Participation Strategy, set up to boost the numbers of adults involved in education and training in order to improve their skills and gain qualifications. The strategies have led to an expansion of learning opportunities as we have seen above. However, admitting to having a literacy 'problem' can still be a source of huge embarrassment for many adults and initial publicity needs to be sensitive and thoughtfully worded. Those learners already on courses will often have useful suggestions about how to draw more people in.

> **Learners at Pecket Well College were planning a residential course for other learners:**
> We wanted the course to be planned by people who themselves have difficulty with reading or writing or have missed out on education for whatever reason... We wanted to make sure that the course catered for the needs of different groups within basic education. So we wrote a letter inviting people to help plan the course. In the letter we said, "Don't worry if you have difficulty reading and writing. We want your ideas and reading and writing are not necessary in the meetings." The letter was a group effort and we were careful to write it in a language that others in basic education would understand.

Publicity needs to give a clear idea of what the benefits of joining a course might be and how it will relate to the learners' particular contexts. Whilst some adults are happy to join a course which focuses solely on literacy skills, many others would prefer to pursue an activity or vocational course where their literacy skills are addressed alongside or embedded within the main area of learning. Many community groups and organisations offer informal and creative learning opportunities that address literacy, language and numeracy needs through art, music, ICT, gardening, photography, health matters and job skills.

Government documents talk about 'hard-to-reach' learners although one small voluntary organisation commented: "It's not the learners who are hard to reach, it's the learning organisations."

The Basic Skills Agency have produced a video entitled 'Reaching Out with Basic Skills' which highlights some of the innovative projects funded under the Adult and Community Learning Fund and the ways in which these projects attracted adults into learning through activities based in a City Farm, a drama project, a young mothers' community centre and a sports centre.
Reaching Out with Basic Skills, video available from the Basic Skills Agency on 0870 600 2400

3 The Adult Literacy Core Curriculum

The Adult Literacy Core Curriculum, published in 2001, is based on the national standards for adult literacy laid down by the government's *Skills for Life* strategy. It describes the content of what should be taught in adult literacy courses wherever they are provided. For the first time, teachers of adult literacy have a document that sets out the skills, knowledge and understanding that they are required to address with their learners.

The Core Curriculum provides a framework for the teaching, but the topics and activities that provide the context for the activities should be based on the interests and the purposes of the learners. Ask yourself what your learners want and need to learn and then map the activities and tasks to the Curriculum.

> **"As far as possible the curriculum should be context free – the core should set out the skills to be taught. The context in which they are taught is a matter for the teacher and learner to decide, particularly as different adults have different motivations."**
> A Fresh Start, February 1999

The national standards on which the Literacy Core Curriculum is based, provide a map of the range of skills and capabilities that adults are expected to need in order to "function and progress at work and in society". The Literacy standards cover the ability to:

- speak, listen and respond
- read and comprehend
- write to communicate

at each of the levels: Entry 1, 2 and 3, Level 1 and Level 2.

Learners at Entry 1 will be beginner readers and writers, who may be getting to grips with writing their names and addresses and reading short texts, whereas Level 2 is judged to be broadly equivalent to GCSE level, grade C. Adult literacy teachers need to be able to use the Core Curriculum to plan and deliver for this full range of ability.

Copies of the Adult Literacy Core Curriculum are available from: The Basic Skills Agency, Admail 524, London WC1A 1BR. Tel: 0870 600 2400.

4 The assessment process

Assessment should be undertaken as part of the 'learning journey' that involves activities undertaken by teachers and learners together. The aim of assessing learners should be to enhance the learning experience and support achievement. It is also a requirement of quality assurance, inspection and funding.

Assessment procedures provide tutors with opportunities to gather information about a learner or group of learners and identify their strengths and areas for development. It also gives the tutor time to understand what the learner brings with them – the many life experiences that will influence how they learn. The information gathered from these activities will help the tutor to plan effective teaching and learning.

The assessment process may vary from setting to setting but one common model for a learner joining an adult literacy programme is as follows:

- screening
- initial assessment before being placed on a literacy course
- diagnostic assessment once the learner is on a course
- ongoing formative assessment throughout a course to inform teaching
- summative assessment at the end of a course or module.

Screening

Screening usually means identifying very broadly whether or not someone needs to improve their literacy skills. This can take place during initial contact with a prospective learner, either in one to one conversation or by information given on an application form by the learner. The positive and welcoming attitudes of frontline staff in an organisation are crucial at this stage in the process as some new learners can very easily be discouraged. New training opportunities exist for staff in this role.

Sometimes screening happens at the same time as initial assessment. Sometimes it occurs as two different phases in the process. There are a number of paper-based and on-line screening tests available to use.

Initial assessment

The purpose of initial assessment activities is to begin to build up a picture of the person, their literacy needs and their own short- and long-term goals. If there is a

Initial assessment tools:
- **The Basic Skills Agency (BSA) has now published a revised version of the initial assessment pack for literacy and numeracy mapped to the national standards for adult literacy and numeracy. Further information is available on the BSA website (www.basic-skills.com).**
- **Cambridge Training and Development (CTAD) have published 'Target Skills' Assessment materials, which is available on their website (www.ctad.com).**
- **West Nottinghamshire College has produced a Keyskillbuilder – see the keyskillbuilder website for further information (www.bksb.co.uk)**

choice of courses on which the learner could be placed, the initial assessment will identify the most appropriate course for them. Initial assessment should be carried out by a qualified teacher wherever possible. This is a process that may be one off, specific and time-bound. It may however, take place over several weeks as you get to know your learners. How long this process takes will depend very much on the context in which you are working.

The process should establish:

- how the learner was referred to your organisation;
- what the potential learner wants to do and why;
- information about their previous educational experiences;
- some information about their previous achievement and skills;
- mother tongue and/or variety of English language used;
- an indication of what their current strengths are;
- an indication of some areas for development;
- issues which may affect their learning, e.g. health problems, dyslexia, work or personal commitments;
- any longer-term goals;
- availability and time constraints;
- an indication of additional support needs.

Initial assessment

"Initial assessment needs to be done with learners rather than to them. It should be of benefit to learners and help them feel positive about themselves and their potential to learn."

"It is important that the process is not seen as part of a deficit model that serves to undermine confidence by focusing only on the things that learners cannot do. Learners need to understand why it is happening and how it can help them."

Green, M. (2003) 'Initial Assessment: a learner-centred process', LSDA p5.

If there is a choice of courses available, you will need to discuss:

- which course would suit them best in terms of timing, location and level;
- what they might expect from the course in terms of size of the group, work being covered;
- whether the course offers a nationally recognised qualification or some other sort of certificate;
- what they might be able to do when they've finished the course.

In the secondary school I was sitting in I got bored. I learned more about general life from the streets. I used to go and help at my brother's or my cousin's fruit and vegetable stall. It gave you a business sense. In secondary school, when we got to the third year, they separated the kids, so the cleverer ones could learn, and the slower ones could stay low.

Adult learner talking about his experiences at school.

Diagnostic assessment

This is a more detailed assessment that should take place once the learner is enrolled onto a course. The aim is to draw up a profile of the learner's strengths and areas for development in more depth than at the initial assessment stage and to map them against the national standards for adult literacy. It is also an opportunity to discuss with a learner the strategies they use, and to explore their learning style. All of this information can be used to inform the Individual Learning Plan (ILP). (See p. 17 Individual Learning Plans)

You can use the *Skills for Life* diagnostic assessment materials that map the learner's skills and abilities against the requirements set out in the national standards and Adult Literacy Core Curriculum. Or you may choose to customise standardised tests or devise ones that are more appropriate for your particular group of learners.

Formative assessment

Good practice in teaching and learning implies ongoing – formative – assessment as well as snapshots at particular times. Formative assessment supports the learning, allowing learners and tutors to check what has been learned and plan future learning. It helps the tutor to see what's going well and what hasn't worked, to know when learners are ready to move on to something new or when to revisit things. It also helps learners to adjust and refine their own targets as strengths and areas for development become better understood.

Formative assessment is not something that should be done once a week or once a month, it can be built in to many of the ongoing day-to-day activities – discussions, questions and answers whether oral or written, reading comprehension, writing tasks, worksheets and spelling games. Encourage learners to engage in self-assessment and peer-assessment whenever possible and involve them in devising tasks and activities for doing this.

Whatever stage of assessment the learner is at, it is important for them to:

- know why they are being assessed;
- know what is being assessed;
- always be assessed against clear criteria;
- be aware that they are entitled to confidential feedback on the findings of the assessment;
- be fully involved in negotiating a plan for their learning that draws on the assessment information.

Try to find a location for assessments that offers the learner a space in which they can talk confidentially if necessary – and try to make the process as informal and relaxed as you can.

Involving the learner
Active involvement can help develop and maintain motivation. Learners need to understand the relevance of what they are learning and recognise its application to real-life activities. They also need to see that they are making progress with the learning and to recognise what they have achieved in order to maintain a sense of success. Ways to help them do this include:

- exploring with learners how they use literacy, language and numeracy skills in everyday life and identifying the particular skills they need to develop to help them clarify the purpose of their learning;
- encouraging learners to apply new learning to real-life activities to ensure skills are maintained.

Planning Learning and Recording Progress and Achievement, DfES 2003, p69

Resources for screening, initial and diagnostic assessment in adult literacy have been developed as part of the *Skills for Life* Strategy. Information on these is available on the readwriteplus website www.dfes.gov.uk/readwriteplus.

Summative assessment

Summative assessment comes at the end of a course or part of a course and sums up the progress made by the learner. This could be in the form of a paper-based or on line test, the presentation of a portfolio or some other form of submission for assessment (see, p. 22).

Record keeping

The Common Inspection Framework requires that you should keep records of each stage of the assessment process. These records should be useful working documents and wherever possible drawn up together with learners and accessible to them (see Section 5: Planning and record keeping, p. 16).

Filling in a record of a first assessment interview is a co-operative process. You may be introducing the learner to scribing – writing her/his words down as accurately as possible and reading them back to check. This is also a key technique for teaching and for making texts to read, out of the words and interests of learners (see language experience approach, p. 37).

5 Planning and record keeping

The DfES publication *Planning Learning and Recording Progress and Achievement: a guide for practitioners* is an excellent resource. It sets out the essential features of good practice for planning learning and recording progress and achievement at each stage of the learning cycle. It also contains good working examples of ILPs, group learning plans and schemes of work. The guide can be ordered free from DfES publications (see appendices for details) and an interactive version is available on www.dfes.gov.uk/readwriteplus.

In order to meet the requirements of funders as well as the Adult Learning Inspectorate (ALI), not only do various processes need to be in place but there should also be *evidence* of good practice. This doesn't necessarily all have to be paper-based, but it does need to demonstrate that your provision and the way it is organised is contributing to learners' achievement. For adult literacy, numeracy and ESOL, evidence of good practice includes the following:

Scheme of work

A scheme of work gives an overview of the literacy topics to be covered during a course and indicates how much time, in terms of sessions or weeks, is to be spent on each topic. The scheme should be mapped to the Adult Literacy Core Curriculum at the appropriate level for the course and reflect the requirements of the accreditation the learners are aiming for (where applicable).

Lesson plans

A lesson plan sets out the main aims and objectives for the lesson and will give a more detailed breakdown of the activities. Lesson plans need to show where tasks and activities are differentiated in order to meet individual language and literacy needs and learning styles.

The lesson plan should include approximate timings for the various activities, as well as notes about what materials and other resources will be needed. It is useful to have a set format but no one size fits all. Find one or devise one that suits your organisation and your learners. Sometimes teachers need to adjust or revise lesson plans in order to respond to things that come up in the session. Provide space for an overall review of how the session went – this need only be brief but is useful when planning your next session. With this in mind, record any changes that took place and make notes of learning points or group interests that can be followed up another time.

Both schemes of work and lesson plans should be useful working documents and not set in stone.

Individual Learning Plans

All learners on Learning and Skills Council (LSC) funded programmes are now expected to have an individual learning plan (ILP) or training plan (ITP) which is drawn up from information that has been gathered from initial and diagnostic assessment. The ILP should be part of and support the process of planning learning and reviewing progress. The outcomes of the ILP process should also inform your scheme of work and lesson plans.

> **"The individual learning plan helps learners know what they are aiming to achieve and by when. Individual negotiation of the plan with their teachers or trainers also increases the involvement of learners, their investment in their own learning and consequently their motivation."**
> *Planning learning and recording progress and achievement: a guide for practitioners,* DfES 2003

Once the ILP has been drawn up with the learner, both teacher and learner should sign it. It should be reviewed and updated at regular intervals, taking into consideration the learner's progress and changing needs. The ILP should be acceptable in terms of the common inspection framework and quality monitoring but it must also be a real *working document* with a clear benefit to both tutor and learner.

Group targets

In some cases it may be appropriate to negotiate a set of shared goals and targets with the group. Once these shared goals have been discussed and agreed with the group, individual goals and targets can then be added. The two sets of goals may be listed separately on the ILP with separate spaces to record when they have been achieved.

Reviewing progress

Regular reviews of ILPs can encourage learners to reflect on their own learning and become more independent learners. Aim to involve learners fully in the process and help them to recognize and record the progress they have made and discuss new targets to be set. If your organisation is being inspected, the inspectors will look at whether learners know what is in their plan and what progress they have made towards achieving their goals and targets.

Tutor records

You should keep records of the following:

- initial assessment;
- diagnostic assessment;
- planning: schemes of work and lesson plans;
- teaching and Learning: ILPs, records of formative assessment, reviews;
- tutorials;
- accreditation and qualification;
- progression.

With all the emphasis on record keeping we need to ensure that it doesn't become too bureaucratic. What is important is that we find ways of making visible to learners the fact that they have made meaningful progress. It is also important to capture and acknowledge the wider benefits of learning, including the unexpected outcomes. For example, new applications of the learning that have been discovered and enjoyed outside of the classroom and so-called 'soft skills', such as gains in confidence and making new friends.

> **"If you have confidence you will try different things, stuff that you wouldn't normally dream of trying. As you get involved in more different experiences you then get even more confident. It's like a spiral and you just need someone to set you off."**
> Learner quoted in *Catching Confidence*, NIACE Report, September 2004

There are a number of ways in which achievement can be recognised, recorded and celebrated. This will depend on the context of the learning and the needs and aims of the learners but will also be influenced by the requirements of funders.

External accreditation

In order to receive guaranteed funding from the LSC, providers require adult literacy learners to be working towards a recognised qualification. A recognised qualification is one that is approved by QCA and is mapped to the national standards for adult literacy. These qualifications are offered by a number of awarding bodies. The *Skills for Life* strategy is funded to ensure that every basic skills learner has an entitlement to free adult literacy (and numeracy and ESOL) learning up to Level 2. There is no time cap on the amount of time needed to achieve these qualifications. Nor is there a requirement to take a nationally-recognised qualification, although funding limitations may dictate this.

External qualifications may recognise evidence of achievement in the form of a portfolio of work and/or internally or externally assessed specific tasks. At Level 1 and Level 2, literacy learners need to take a national test in order to gain a nationally recognised qualification.

For information on all the approved qualifications for post-16 literacy and numeracy learners, including the National Tests, go to the DfES website: www.dfes. gov.uk/readwriteplus/LearningInfrastructure.

Move On and Learndirect
The Move On Project, funded by the DfES, works to support organisations and encourages more adults to brush up on their English and maths skills in order to achieve a national qualification at Level 1 and Level 2. They provide taster sessions for learners, short brush-up courses and briefing sessions for staff on the tests and how to become a test centre. A core resource is the National Test Toolkit, available from DfES publications (tel. 0845 60 222 60) or as downloads from the Move On website: www.move-on.org.uk.

Learndirect also offer the National Tests online as well as short courses to prepare for them. Information is available on: www.learndirect.co.uk.

The national tests

There is concern among adult literacy practitioners that the primary skills covered in the national tests at Level 1 and Level 2 are reading and comprehension. Because the answers are multiple choice there is very little writing required and the test alone does not reflect a learner's real abilities.

Although LSC funding is tied to these qualifications, they may not be suitable for all learners. Learners who are dyslexic, bilingual learners and speakers of non-standard varieties of English and those who tend to panic in test situations may well be deterred by this form of assessment. Achievement funding attached to tests can be problematic in that it can encourage teaching to the tests, rather than building real understanding, and focusing on the needs and interests of the learners.

Two excellent discussion papers that contribute to the debate on testing and national achievement targets are:

- *Testing, Testing…1, 2, 3: Assessment in adult literacy, language and numeracy,* **Peter Lavender, Jay Derrick and Barry Brooks, a NIACE Discussion Paper, 2004**
- *Literacy and Social Inclusion: the policy challenge. A discussion Paper.* **Viv Bird, National Literacy Trust**

It is important, if adult literacy learners are to be engaged in and enthused about learning beyond the short term, that their real needs and motivations are addressed and that achievement is seen in broader terms than the gaining of the recognised qualification. For this reason, NIACE has worked with the LSC to draw up a robust framework for recording and recognising progress and achievement in non-accredited learning (RARPA – see below).

Non-accredited learning

Many learners make great progress whilst on a literacy course, but for a number of reasons may not be in a position or wish to claim externally accredited achievement through a qualification. This does not mean that their achievements and progress should go unrecorded. There have been many developments in recognising and recording progress and achievement in non-accredited learning. Both the LSC's Recognising and Recording Progress and Achievement (RARPA) project and the DfES Skills for Life Planning Learning and Recording Progress and Achievement Guide (PLRA) explore ways that non-accredited learning can be identified and recorded.

- *Planning Learning and Recording Progress and Achievement* **(ref PLRA1) available free from the DfES (see appendices)**
- **For information about RARPA go to: www.lsc.gov.uk, search for RARPA.**

Measuring progress

> "There was most satisfaction with progress where learners were actively engaged with tutors in the processes of planning content and recognising learning gain. The journey metaphor with its language of travel and movement, was particularly effective in unlocking the capacity of learners to discuss their views on the pace of learning and progress."
>
> *Learning Journeys: Learners' voices: a research report on learners' views on progress and achievement in literacy and numeracy* by Jane Ward with Judith Edwards (2002), LSDA

Assessment activities on their own don't always tell us how much progress a learner is making. Learners need to be involved in discussions about their progress, for example, in group or individual tutorials and, if necessary, supported to find ways of articulating their goals, their aims and their achievements. For some learners, progress may be in very small steps but this still needs to be acknowledged.

'Other' goals and achievements

Literacy tutors and learners often talk about achievements that can be identified which were not even planned; these include increases in confidence, improved speaking and listening skills and changes in attitude or social awareness. Even though they were unanticipated they should still be recorded as they are important outcomes of involvement in a learning activity. For instance, a learner may come in to class with a story about an achievement at home or work: write it down and put it in their file.

What counts as evidence for achievement?

Work folders/portfolios, computer records, audio and videotapes, photographs and free writing can all provide evidence that learners have achieved their learning goals.

Celebrating achievement

Whether or not learners have achieved a nationally recognised qualification, it's important, and fun, to celebrate the progress they have made. Here are some tried and tested ideas:

- Hold an award ceremony for learners to be presented with their certificate (invite a celebrity to present them and provide food if you can or ask for food and drink to share);
- Produce a book of student writing – prose and poetry/international recipes/hot household tips;
- Organise a reading evening – ask learners to read out their favourite piece of their own writing;
- Organise a trip – or even better a weekend away to write (this can serve as a celebration as well as stimulus for further writing).

The first reason we wrote this book was for ourselves – to remember our lives and our history. We lived our memories again as we talked and wrote, and we will remember whenever we read this book.
Dawan Miyi Iyo Magaalo (Our Strength Comes with Us): Somali Women's Voices. Somali Women's Association, Tower Hamlets, 1987

Summative review

As part of their final or summative review, learners should be encouraged to think about what they might do next. However, information about possible progression opportunities should be made available throughout the learning programme so that the interests and aspirations of learners can be identified and discussed. Learning providers should consider what progression routes are available within their own organisation as well as that on offer from other providers in the area and through routes such as online learning.

Information and advice (IAG)

Some learners will need to consolidate their learning at one level in order to build confidence and competence. Others will progress up a learning ladder towards their longer-term goals and ambitions. Importantly, tutors must create time to share information and offer advice and, where necessary, bring in colleagues who are qualified in providing Information, Advice and Guidance (IAG).

Progression

Literacy progression for learners could include:

- a move to the next level, e.g. from an Entry 3 group to a Level 1 group;
- a sideways move in to another course;
- further discrete literacy focused programmes e.g. GCSE, Move On;
- vocational or workplace learning with further literacy support or embedded literacy;
- leisure learning programmes – which further develop literacy skills e.g. creative writing;
- paid or voluntary work;
- a new activity for which literacy is a springboard: learning to drive, joining a community group, travelling to an unfamiliar destination.

6 Good practice in the classroom

Good practice involves effective planning, assessment processes and record keeping which inform and contribute to the development and management of teaching and learning. Adult literacy learners should be actively involved in planning and reviewing their learning. Ensuring that the contexts for learning are relevant to their lives and needs is essential for building confidence and motivation.

Good practice in teaching and learning requires an in-depth understanding of the Adult Literacy Core Curriculum and how to use this framework to provide a relevant and purposeful experience for learners. It also needs to be supportive and enjoyable too!

The learning environment

In many smaller organisations it's not always possible to have a choice of where the teaching will take place. However, try to make sure that the environment is comfortable and welcoming:

- display relevant and eye-catching posters on the wall. (If you display learners' own writing, enlarge the print to make it easily readable and ensure it's attractive to look at.)
- keep a range of worksheets, reading books and newspapers or magazines available and accessible for learners to use. They don't all have to be at current reading levels.
- arrange tables and chairs to maximise possibilities for whole group work and rearrange them if you want people to work in small groups or pairs. Try to ensure that learners don't have their backs to each other, particularly for discussions.

Group dynamics

Establishing a supportive, welcoming group atmosphere right from the start is vital. Use ice-breaker activities so that learners can get to know each other. Promote collaboration, not competition and respect for each other as learners and as adults who have experience of life to share.

A good literacy course should provide a balance of whole group, small group, pair and individual work. Although beginner learners will need a lot of one-to-one attention, plan in opportunities for learners to interact, to collaborate and help each other. Group work that is well structured promotes teamwork and emphasises that each person has something to teach and learn from each other.

INSPIRATIONS

Interchill/Hurricane Films Project (Northwest)

This ACLF-funded project took the form of a community workshop to develop a script and produce a low-budget film based on the group's own experiences. The group of young people involved in the project discussed characters, debated stories and worked together on improving scenes for the film collaboratively before actually writing the script. This innovative approach to developing writing skills allowed the group time to process the information and ideas they needed to create the script.

Tanya – a group member comments: "Since attending the script workshops I have learned how to write simple things, such as stage directions, and I have learned the more difficult side such as writing dialogue and having to look at a script for the audience's point of view… I am now trying to write my own short films…"

From On the Case: Studies from the ACLF (NIACE 2004)

Structuring the session

It's a good idea to have a short fun activity or some revision task for learners as they come in and settle down. The Literacy Core Curriculum encourages the integration of skills, so try to provide a balance of activities – reading, writing, speaking and listening. Discuss with your group whether they would like to set aside a particular time-slot for spelling work. Keep an eye on timings and pace – don't rush people but be aware of the different time it might take them to do things.

Structure sessions coherently:

- Begin by recalling the previous session – ask learners what they can remember and what they learnt.
- Introduce the present session by explaining how it will build on the previous session.
- Explain what you intend to cover in the session and why. Say what you hope will have been achieved by the end of the session in terms of learning.

- At the end of the activity or before moving on to something different, recap and check progress and understanding.
- At the end of the session, recap on what has been covered and review whether what you set out to teach has been learned.
- Give an indication of what you hope to cover next time.

Don't assume that your learners will know what you're trying to teach them. You need to be explicit about your aims, your objectives and how the activities will support them in their learning. This involves sharing and using the language you use to label and describe literacy activities, e.g. what is a draft?

Key resources in the classroom
- Whiteboard and different coloured pens
- Lined A4 paper with margin
- Plastic or wooden 3D letters
- Tape recorder
- Overhead projector
- Notebooks (as personal dictionaries or for rough drafts)
- Pens and pencils
- Scrap paper
- Learner dictionaries (see end of the Lifeline: Tutor resources and teaching materials)
- Books: easy-readers, novels, poetry, short stories and reference books

Choosing learning materials and resources
Thankfully there are a much wider range of materials for adult literacy teaching available these days (see end of the Lifeline: Tutor resources and teaching materials). Many experienced practitioners however find that these 'off the shelf' resources are potentially useful but often have to be adapted to suit the needs and interests of their particular learners.

The materials and resources you choose have to be effective in supporting learner progress. They should:

- be designed for adults – don't use children's texts and workbooks unless this reflects a learner's aims of reading to or helping children;
- reflect the cultural identities and experiences of your learners;
- involve tasks and activities set within meaningful and relevant contexts;
- be clear about their purpose and how to use them;
- clearly indicate the skill(s) to be developed;
- support a range of learning styles;
- be structured to ensure clear differentiation and progression between levels.

The best resource for stimulating discussion, reading and writing may be the environment and community around you. Take learners out if you can – visit parks, places of historic and contemporary interest, museums and art galleries.

Developing good study skills

- Encourage learners to keep their work well organised in a folder or notebook. Not only will this contribute to effective study habits and reviewing work done, but it will also help learners to see for themselves where they have made progress.
- Foster independent learning wherever possible – negotiate homework tasks, re-reading a text, learning five spellings, re-drafting written work or doing some personal research.
- Encourage punctuality and regular attendance and negotiate a shared group ethos on this.
- Support learners in setting targets and goals for themselves.
- Provide opportunities for learners to explore their learning style and understand the strategies that work best for them.
- Teach alphabetical order to support and develop research skills.

Encourage learners to get in to the habit of completing a brief record sheet or lesson diary at the end of the lesson, with help if necessary, indicating briefly what they have done and which tasks have been completed or need more time. This can be combined with a note of any homework set.

Differentiation

Differentiation is about being able to draw on a range of techniques and approaches to support learning and introduce activities and materials that take into account learners' individual differences, e.g. preferred learning style, level of skill, language use, previous experience and knowledge, interests and aspirations. Some examples of differentiation practices are:

- discuss learning styles with learners – how do they learn best? By seeing, listening or doing?;
- support learners to find the strategies that work best for them and also to explore new ways of working;
- ensure activities are varied so that different ways of learning can be addressed, e.g. listen to tapes as well as read from a text;
- provide a range of tasks on a worksheet and encourage learners to pick and choose;
- devise extension activities such as some free writing or research for those learners who may finish before others;
- encourage peer support and help.

Using ICT

The subject of using ICT in literacy classrooms deserves a booklet of its own. Tutors in literacy, numeracy and ESOL work, as in other fields of adult education are increasingly being expected to use ICT in their teaching.

Certainly, access to computer facilities, particularly if there is an internet connection, opens up many new possibilities.

There are many creative and imaginative ways of using ICT to enhance learning. ICT can help learners develop their writing, reading and spelling. Proof-reading skills can be honed and for some students, editing can be a far simpler process than on paper. It is worth remembering though that the amount of text on an average web page can present significant difficulties for many new readers and skills necessary for navigating web pages and making the best use of facilities such as the spelling and grammar checks need to be explicitly taught.

Once learners have gained confidence, a range of activities can be pursued, such as:

- using CD ROMs to develop research and writing skills;
- using interactive multimedia to enhance a range of writing activities, e.g. producing a poster or advert;
- using the Internet and other web resources.

ICT can provide opportunity for learners to practise and reinforce skills in a variety of interactive exercises that provide instant feedback (though it can be very frustrating to know that you have got something wrong without knowing why!).

There is an ever-growing list of useful interactive websites for learners to access. Although many of these are intended for children rather than adults, it is well worth picking through them as many of them have plenty of materials suitable for adults as well, including many excellent interactive games and puzzles. It is a good idea to ask learners to evaluate particular sites. Suggested websites can be found in the Reference section at the end of this guide.

A useful resource for ICT teaching is *Using laptop computers to develop basic Skills; a handbook for practitioners* (available free from the Basic Skills Agency). This publication contains practical advice and ideas about using laptops and developing and using ICT. There are example materials, mapped to the Literacy and Numeracy Core Curricula, and an accompanying CD-ROM with hyperlinks to other sites.

Working with bilingual learners

Increasing numbers of learners on adult literacy courses will be bilingual or multi-lingual speakers who speak English fluently enough to participate actively in the group. For many highly qualified other language speakers, an adult literacy course is probably not appropriate and a course which can address their English language needs in the context of employment or preparation for employment in their area of expertise may serve their purposes better.

Some suggestions to get started:

- A pilot interactive version of the Adult ESOL Core Curriculum is available on the DfES website: dfes.gov.uk/curriculum_esol/
- Get on to the NATECLA News mailing list and go to events if you can
- Work with qualified ESOL tutors if you can and seek more specialist support from your local FE college, adult learning centre or Professional Development Centre if you have one.
- London Online is a combined project and course. It is part of an initiative to train ESOL teachers paired with multimedia developers from further and adult community education to produce online interactive ESOL materials.

See also: *The power of writing, the writing of power: approaches to adult ESOL writing*, Elsa Auerbach, Language Issues, Vol 14, No1)

Checklist of teaching strategies
- Use strategies that will accommodate different learning styles.
- Provide a balance of reading, writing, spelling, speaking and listening activities.
- Introduce new topics and activities clearly – explain why you are doing them.
- Provide a mix of whole group, small group and pair work.
- Try to give individual attention to learners on a fair and regular basis.
- Use active questioning techniques and ask open questions, such as 'What do you know about...?' 'What do you think happens next...?' 'Why do you think this is...?' etc.
- Encourage learners to explore ideas and problems rather than giving them the answers straight away.

- Encourage students right from the start to think about writing as a process – help them to develop skills of drafting, proof reading and editing.
- Provide good models of texts that you want learners to produce.
- Foster critical reading skills.

7 Developing writing skills

Why is writing difficult?

Research into adult literacy has shown that writing and spelling generally cause more difficult than reading. Writing is harder than speaking or reading because the writer has to get across exactly what they mean and make it interesting. This means having thought about who is reading what you write. Generating a text requires a high level of skill. Sounds and letters have to be matched accurately to form words and the correct words have to be chosen, grammar and punctuation must be organised accurately and the overall meaning of the text has to be clear and appropriate for the purpose. Trying to do all of this can distract you from working out what you really want to say.

In addition, many adult learners speak a non-standard variety of English. While Standard English is the dominant form of public communication, it is not the way in which most people speak. So the gap between speaking and writing can present even more of a challenge.

One way of bridging the gap is by scribing – writing down, with the learner's agreement, something that she or he says. This may be a small but memorable comment or a short personal account of experience or feelings. This can then go into the learner's file.

It is possible, even with learners at Entry level one, to have discussions about why writing is so different from speaking and why some formal styles of writing have more status than others. Reading and writing personal language histories, reading about and discussing the development of English and how languages change over time, comparing standard and non-standard forms of writing can all help to raise learners' awareness of issues of language variety and support them in developing writing skills.

Good practice involves:

- Providing lively, relevant activities to stimulate writing and encouraging lots of discussion.
- Explicitly modelling writing tasks and providing good examples.
- Emphasising writing as a process – drafting, proof-reading and editing.
- Providing opportunities for creative writing – prose and poetry.
- Encouraging collaborative working and sharing ideas.
- Providing effective feedback on drafts which allow learners to develop their

ideas, style and tone as well as improve spelling, punctuation and grammar.
- Allowing enough time for writing and supporting learners in extended writing as they progress.
- Helping with structure by the use of writing frames, models and other approaches.
- The celebration of written work, for example by sharing it with others.

Keeping it real

Rather than choosing tasks/activities that bear no relation to the lives of the learners completing them, contextualise tasks and activities to reflect learners lives and interests. In the case of letter writing, this might mean that learners are encouraged to think about the kind of letters they might need to write e.g. letters to a housing association, letters to school or job application enquiries. Read and discuss typical letters sent by the local authority or companies and encourage learners to bring in letters they have received themselves. Discuss what makes an effective letter and how best to reply. This in turn could lead to work around lobbying and campaigning about local issues. This could be extended to the use of the internet and other ways of communicating via new technology.

INSPIRATIONS

A tutor working on writing on letters of complaint with her group brought in a two-tier In-tray with the drawers marked URGENT and NON-URGENT. She asked them to imagine that the tray was sitting on the desk of a council official who had to reply to the letters. A scenario was produced by the group around the demand for a play area to be built on their estate. The group then discussed what was needed to get a letter in to the URGENT tray. All of the ideas came from the group – a strong, clear message about the problem and description of its impact, a demand for a time-limited, specific response to the problem and a suggestion of further action the writer might take if the demand was not met. The group also were very clear that the letter needed to be in a formal style, appropriately laid out, polite but firm and preferably typed or word-processed. The tutor then supported the group by providing a model for the lay out and structure, with a choice of phrases and with spelling – but the letters came from the group!

Different types of writing

Learners need to grow confident enough to apply the literacy skills they are learning to a variety of contexts. You may need to begin with writing tasks that are familiar for learners, e.g. making lists, leaving notes, writing birthday cards and informal letters or practical and useful activities such as making insurance claims.

Share the language that names these different purposes for writing and discuss the way that style, tone, layout, language use, degree of formality/informatlity will vary according to the purpose. Extend the range of writing to include the following:

- autobiographical writing and reminiscing or reflecting on feelings and opinions about a whole range of subjects;
- creative writing activities such as writing poetry, fiction or writing for children are often extremely liberating and satisfying for learners and can lead to a discussion of varied forms and conventions around writing;
- writing for work-related tasks, such as reports, minutes, and memos introduces learners to another range of formats and styles and can often draw on techniques developed through other tasks.

Home and family

If my son was a bird he would be a robin redbreast
If he was a flower he would be a daffodil
If he was a piece of furniture he would be a table
If he was a vegetable he would be tomatoes
If he was a building he would be a church
He would be reggae music
He would be sea water
He would be a pineapple plantation
He would be an orange
He would be a gate
He would be a running track

Link writing to the reading of a range of texts (see Section 8: Developing Reading Skills).

Drafting, proof-reading and editing

Learners should always be encouraged to draft and proof-read their writing. Beginner writers will need lots of support with this initially. Learners often lack confidence around checking their own work particularly if their education has been traditional and teacher centred. Encourage peer support wherever you can.

- read sentences aloud to check for meaning;
- use a dictionary to check for context as well as the correct spelling (the necessary skills such as understanding alphabetical order need to be explicitly taught and practised);
- teach higher level learners how to use a Thesaurus and choose alternative words;
- elicit alternative words from beginner writers and leave it to them to choose;
- pair people up to check and respond to each others work – with their agreement!;
- discuss and draw up with learners a checklist for proof reading and self-correcting – use the checklist to focus on one thing at a time, e.g. overall meaning, spelling, punctuation, layout, etc.

Giving feedback on written work

Try and provide oral and written feedback on learners' work:

- Be encouraging and positive about the first draft.
- Focus on two or three learning points you want them to address – some recurring spelling mistakes, a couple of examples of wrong word order or where you feel they could add a bit more detail. Don't overload them.
- Where a point is being made in the writing that is not clear, identify this for the learner and encourage them to find ways of making the point more clearly. Paired reading of a draft and talking it through can be very helpful.
- If a spelling mistake is about leaving off the 's' on a plural or 'ed' in a past tense, help the learner to find the error by reminding them about rules, e.g. "How do we usually show that a word is a plural, or more than one?" "What ending do you need for a word in the past tense?".
- If possible ask them to identify errors, assess how effective the piece is, what they think they might like to change (with learners at higher levels you can ask them to do this before you look at their work).
- Avoid giving learners lots of new words and phrases that they might not use themselves – check that they feel comfortable with the wording.
- Many learners have had negative experiences of teachers writing all over their work in red pen. Using a pencil or some other coloured pen is a good idea – again, consult your learners on what they feel comfortable with.
- Make notes of where learners are making errors, to follow up in future sessions.

Writing frames

Writing frames are a way of helping learners to develop more independent writing skills. An example would be a task sheet that provides sentence openings for completion or a letter format that gives the layout, salutation, opening sentence and closing phrase.

To be used effectively, writing frames need to:

(a) **offer enough support to help the learner attempt a new or difficult task but not so much that the writing is reduced to filling in boxes;**

(b) **be used as part of the planning and drafting stages, helping learners marshal their thoughts and organise what they want to write;**

(c) **be properly structured to suit the type of text and style of writing being practised;**

(d) **be designed and used progressively, providing less support for harder tasks as learners gain in experience and skill;**

(e) **be used alongside reading texts that model the type of writing being practised.**

Adapted from: Adult Literacy Core Curriculum

Development and practice of handwriting skills

Beginner writers may well have to practice letter formation and writing on and between the lines. Simple techniques for holding the pen or positioning the paper can make a huge difference to these learners and to others who have lost confidence in or feel unhappy with their handwriting. The use of ICT can be wonderfully liberating for some adults who really struggle with their handwriting, but for many others being unfamiliar with a keyboard and mouse can bring further problems and defeats.

There are lots of handwriting practice workbooks on the market, but most are produced for children. Choose carefully!

NIACE Write Where You Are Campaign
The NIACE Write Where You Are campaign inspired adults to write about their lives and their interests in creative, imaginative and fun ways. The campaign helped adults strengthen their reading and writing skills and also encouraged people who didn't think they could write to have a go.

As well as information about the campaign, the website includes a wealth of inspiring teaching resources to support literacy teaching and writers' workshops. To download the materials go to: www.niace.org.uk/ALW/writewhereyouare/Teaching Writing

8 Developing reading skills

Experienced readers use a number of strategies to get at the meaning in texts. We use:

- what we already know about a topic or text to help us make overall sense;
- our knowledge of how punctuation works and how sentences are put together;
- recognition of whole words, letters and shapes;
- our knowledge of sounds and spellings.

Reading is not a passive process. It involves problem solving, active prediction (guessing), searching and an ability to use past knowledge and experience to make sense of what we are reading. To help learners improve their reading, teachers need to help them to draw on all of these different strategies.

Here are just a few ideas for working on reading with your learners, but there are lots more to draw on!

Choosing and simplifying texts

All readers need to have texts to read that are interesting and relevant to their lives and this is particularly so for beginner readers. There are a lot of excellent collections of student writing available. Local and national newspapers are also a good source of topical and often controversial articles. It may be necessary to simplify texts to make them accessible to your learners.

Prediction

When introducing a reading text to learners begin with questions and discussion that will encourage learners to share what they already know about the topic and begin to predict the content. You can use a headline, a picture or some key words and ask the question 'What do you know about this?'. This can contribute enormously to learners' confidence and successful reading of the text.

Language experience approach – for beginner readers

Language experience allows you to draw on a learner's own experiences and interests. By writing down their stories and ideas you can create reading material that uses familiar language and where the content is relevant and known to them.

This helps learners to read for meaning right from the start. They gain confidence quickly, as the words on the page are their own.

1. **Begin by discussing with the student what they would like to write about.**
2. **Write down what the student says, word for word. Use a clear, large, cursive script with capital letters as appropriate. Say each word as you write it. Keep it short, perhaps only one sentence for a real beginner reader.**
3. **Read the story back to the learner. Do not correct grammar or choice of words but ask if the learner wants to make any changes.**
4. **Read it over to the learner two or three times, encouraging them to join in with you when they feel comfortable to do so.**

You can then use the text to develop reading by:

- working on key personally-relevant words – matching words on cards to words in the text;
- building a sight vocabulary of frequently used words, e.g. a, the, and, I, of, was etc.;
- sequencing words and sentences.

The language experience approach works not only because it uses words that have special meaning for learners, but it also uses their vocabulary and language patterns, helping to bridge that gap between spoken and written English.

Having gained in confidence, learners will also need to read different kinds of text of an interesting nature, pitched at the appropriate level.

Promoting initial reading skills (for beginner readers)

It is important to find or produce reading texts that contain familiar words. Repetition of words or words which contain similar sound patterns (sing, ring, fling, string) will build confidence and reduce anxiety. Support learners in their reading by working with them on:

- building a sight vocabulary of key words;
- developing alphabetic knowledge – this means knowing what sounds the letters make, including the sounds made by combinations of letters such as 'pl' or 'br' (see Phonics, on following page);
- plurals – how they change according to regular and irregular forms;
- recognising tenses – simple past, present and future;
- building up words – showing how root words can be changed by the use of prefixes and suffixes (happy – unhappy; work – working);
- recognising the shape of words – this is a very useful multi-sensory skills that encourages learners to 'draw' and visualize words;

- using rhyme and sound recognition;
- learning common spelling patterns.

Developing reading skills

When listening to a learner read the tutor should begin to make an assessment about the kind of problems that the learner might be experiencing. Are they unsure about the sound the initial letters make, or the ending? Have they confused the word with another? Are they rushing and not paying attention to parts of the word? Most learners want clear feedback on how their reading is progressing with some practical strategies to support further improvement. Reading activities for more confident readers should seek to develop a variety of techniques. These include:

- **skimming** – this is a kind of speed reading that gives one the overall impression of the text. (Do I want to read this? What's it about? Is it of interest?);
- **scanning** – this technique involves looking though a text quickly while searching for a particular piece of information (telephone directories, dictionaries, contents' pages, etc.);
- **close reading** – this is a careful, intensive form of reading that one might use for narratives, textbooks and focused study;
- **reading a variety of texts** – this gives learners an opportunity to establish an understanding of purpose and audience in writing in addition to the very specialised use of technical vocabulary and graphical material that they will come across in everyday reading matter;
- **critical reading** – encourage learners to ask questions of the texts they read: Who wrote it? Why? Do I agree/disagree with it? Do I think it's good/interesting/right? Expect them to have opinions and ideas about what they read.

Assess whether or not a learner is reading for meaning. Understanding what they are reading, even if they make mistakes, is more important than technical accuracy.

Allow time for discussions that not only concern content, but have regard to the kinds of language, stylistic features and syntax that the texts use. Read novels and extracts, short stories, poems, formal and informal letters, diaries, textbooks, reference books, manuals, leaflets, flyers, newspapers, magazines, reviews and cartoons. The list is endless but whatever you choose, ensure it is topical, interesting and relevant to your learners and their lives.

Cloze

A cloze text is one where words have been deleted and a space left for the learner to insert an appropriate word. It is a not a good idea, particularly if you are working with beginner readers, to delete words randomly from a text. Use the cloze activity to reinforce knowledge of social sight words or key words that are relevant for a particular topic or activity. For self-checking purposes put the words to be inserted in the text into a box at the bottom of the worksheet.

For more advanced readers, you can use cloze activities to encourage the prediction of words that will "make sense" in the text. Try not to be too prescriptive, encourage variety as long as the meaning is not lost, as this will also help learners to build their written vocabulary.

Phonics

Phonic reading schemes are based on the repetitious use of sounds in words that have a regular spelling pattern – think: *the cat sat on the mat*. For many learners this method of learning may bring back memories of trying to learn to read at school and their subsequent failure to do so. While phonic and decoding techniques are still an important part of how children and adults can be taught to read, they no longer predominate in the way they once did; rather they are useful as one of a number of cues to help make sense of new words. Unfortunately there are very few phonic reading schemes written for adults, most of them are written for children. There is evidence that a well-structured, interesting and adult phonic reading scheme can help some beginner readers who may have missed out on this stage of their learning. Looking for patterns of sound and letter groups also helps with spelling.

Reading aloud in the group

As long as a group feel safe with each other, you can ask them to volunteer to read aloud. It's a good idea to agree some ground rules first, e.g. not interrupting, how to deal with errors, when to ask for help, etc. Vary whole group reading sessions with small group and paired reading which encourages collaborative working, helps learners to develop listening skills more effectively. This also provided a more comfortable space for those quieter students who don't like to read aloud in a large group.

If a reader is struggling with a word, encourage them to draw on the strategies that work for them:

- What's the beginning sound in the word? (*phonics*)
- Can you think of another word that looks like this one? (*sight vocabulary*)
- You've got the right beginning but look at the ending again. (*rules/grammar*)
- What do you think the word might be? What would make sense in this sentence? (*prediction*)

9 Teaching spelling

There are a vast number of books, work packs and other online resources that are now available for tutors to use to help learners with spelling. It is wise to avoid those written specifically for children because the vocabulary is often not relevant to adult learners' lives.

It is useful to build spelling into a session in a structured way. You might want to set aside 15 or 20 minutes each session to work on specific spelling patterns, to revise words already learnt or to introduce new strategies for learning spellings. You will also need to address spelling issues as they arise. Encourage learners to identify words that are important to them that they want to learn to spell and build up a vocabulary bank of key words for the group. Many learners enjoy having their own personal dictionary in which they can record words they've learnt.

INSPIRATIONS

Tutors working on a work-based learning project with Transport for London produced a really useful pocket-sized spelling book with learners that was very popular. The book contained pages of common words – days of the week, months of the year, useful key words and also some blank pages for the learners' own words as well as space to record sentences they might need for work, e.g. delays on the Circle Line.

Don't spend too long going over and over spellings – it can become boring and tiring! Also words learnt need to be used in context. Give Entry-level learners short cloze sentences that they complete with the words they have learnt. More confident writers can use the words in sentences of their own.

Spelling strategies

The ways in which learners can be helped to develop spelling are known as 'word attack strategies'. These involve employing a variety of cues to help decode (read) and encode (write) words:

Using visual strategies

Identify the difficult part of the word and highlight it or box it in felt tip:

- rec ei ve   gover n ment   wr iting.
- Find words within words: cap-a-city sign-post foot-ball.
- Look carefully at the shape of the word: bed hospital college

Note: it is important to use lower case letters when you are writing a word you want to learn, as by writing in capitals you lose the individual shape of the word.

Strategies which draw on sound-symbol relationships (auditory cues)

- Change the sound of the word. Exaggerate the pronunciation or say it in a funny way: *wed-nes-day   rasp-berry   to-get-her.*
- Say the names of the letters in rhythm: *p-e o-p l-e   q-u e-u e.*
- Split words into syllables and beat out the syllables as you say the words.
- Use tapes of songs.
- Group words with similar sounds, e.g. *cool, roots, boom.*

Strategies that draw on knowledge of word meanings and roots

Learning about the derivations of words. Many words in English have their roots in other languages, either because of invasion into the country in the past, because of British colonialism or more recently because of the spread of American language and the development of technology:

- For example, television: '*tele*' comes from a Greek word meaning from afar or over a distance; '*visio*' means sight in Latin.
- Learning about prefixes, suffixes and root words:
  E.g. *un-* meaning *not* – *un*likely, *un*loved, *un*certain
        -ful meaning *full of* – dread*ful*, beauti*ful*, care*ful*.
- Knowledge of comparatives and superlatives, such as *thin, thinner, thinnest.*

- Learning about common endings which usually indicate what sort of word group the word belongs to:
  E.g. *-ed* endings on verbs (worked, played, called)
      -ly endings on adverbs (truly, madly, deeply)
      -al endings on adjectives (casual, medical, gradual).
- Knowledge that many question words being 'wh', e.g. *why, what, when, where, who, which.*
- Knowledge of silent letters and the historical reason for them, such as knife, knight, knee, knock – in medieval times the 'k' was pronounced aloud.

Kinaesthetic strategies

- Trace the letters with your forefinger as you say or visualise the word.
- Use wooden letters and move them about to spell the word.
- Make the shapes of the letters with your fingers, hands or even your body.
- Write big.

Look, say, cover, write, check (LSCWC)

This is a method of learning spellings that really works if it is used regularly and in combination with the other strategies that have been mentioned. Discuss different strategies and help learners to clarify what strategies work best for them depending on whether they are mainly visual, auditory or kinaesthetic learners. Encourage learners to use this method regularly but only practise five or six words at the most. It helps to learn words that have some personal relevance or which have similar patterns or roots. Avoid grouping spellings to be learnt that may be confusing, e.g. to, too, two

LOOK at the correct spelling? Try to photograph it in your mind: pay attention to any difficult/unfamiliar parts and highlight them or write this part in a different colour pen.

SAY the word out loud: if necessary, pronounce it to emphasise the spelling e.g. Wed-nes-day.

COVER the word and try and visualise it.

WRITE out the word in lower-case letters without looking back at the original.

CHECK – Compare the version with original. If correct, well done. If not, try again.

Encourage learners to practise their spellings at home every couple of days.

Other techniques and strategies for more confident spellers:

- Mnemonics. These are memory tricks for helping to learn spellings which are difficult to remember:
  - rhythm – **h**as **y**our **t**wo **h**ips **m**oving
  - you h**ear** with your **ear**s
  - Necessary – It is ne**cess**ary to have one **c**ollar and two **s**ocks

  And almost everyone knows **i** before **e** except after **c** (but be careful because there are exceptions!).
- Use dictionaries/spell checkers and word lists. There are now lots of good dictionaries for adult literacy learners – choose carefully and encourage learners to find a dictionary that they feel comfortable with.
- Learn spelling rules and exceptions.

Spelling tests

Some learners love spelling tests, for others they are a harrowing reminder of school days. Regular spelling tests can be useful for following up words learned after practising with LSCWC but never force learners to participate. Limit the number of words to test to a maximum of six for beginner readers and writers and ten for more confident learners. Spelling tests should be set in the context of an additional strategy for learning spellings and self-checking, not as a competition, unless you are certain that each individual wants it to be so.

Games

Learning should be fun and games can provide an opportunity to encourage group cohesion and break down barriers between learners:

- Scrabble;
- Crosswords;
- Countdown (as seen on TV);
- Constantinople (see how many new words can be made by choosing and re-arranging letters in a given word or word, e.g. from Constantinople: tin son, place, stop etc. Students will be amazed how quickly you can get up to 50 words or more);
- Word pairs (pelmanism);
- I Spy (good for learning initial letters and sounds);
- Hangman, or a version of it – you need to be sensitive to learners who may become to the UK having witnessed traumatic events in their own countries.

10 Speaking and listening activities

Although good literacy teaching has always included lots of opportunities for discussion and listening activities, it was only with the introduction of the Literacy Core Curriculum that this area of work was identified as an area to be explicitly addressed in literacy teaching. There are at least two good reasons for this. First, most of us shape meaning in speech or in 'inner speech' in our heads before we write it down – it's the raw material. Second, we learn about different types, styles and ranges of languages – different discourses – from using speech in social contexts. In writing we have to internalise these differences and apply them to the solitary activity of writing.

The challenge for tutors is to find contexts for the development of these skills that acknowledge adult experiences and which avoid being patronising. A learner at Entry level 1 in their reading and writing skills may nevertheless be an articulate and forceful speaker. Providing the contexts for this work are negotiated with learners, many adults are happy to work on speaking and listening skills as a means to develop confidence in specific situations.

Establish grounds rules with learners in the group about their ideas of the most effective ways of communicating, such as not interrupting, taking turns to speak, showing respect and active listening.

Ideas that have been used successfully include:

- Storytelling – drawing on folk tales and oral traditions;
- Mock or real meetings where decisions have to be agreed on, e.g. should we introduce a regular timed tea break in this class?;
- Presentations of arguments for and against;
- Role-plays where learners can 'try out' a number of roles, e.g. chair, advocate, antagonist;
- Speaking to the group about a hobby or interest;
- Dramatising an event into a short, maybe improvised, play (video or tape to help you and your learners review and develop).

If you can tape-record speaking activities – with permission, of course – you will have a further set of texts, generated by learners, to work with for reading, writing and spelling.

11 Additional support for adult literacy learners

The Disability Discrimination Act (DDA) was passed in 1995 to introduce new measures aimed at ending the discrimination which many disabled people face. The Act was extended to education from September 2002. Governing bodies of FE colleges and Local Education Authorities (LEAs) are named as responsible bodies which have duties under this legislation:

- not to treat disabled students less favourably for a reason related to their disability, and
- to provide reasonable adjustments for disabled learners.

A key purpose of initial and diagnostic assessment (in addition to identifying learning aims) is to identify learners' additional support needs. These may include the need to provide support for specific learning difficulties affecting literacy such as dyslexia, dyspraxia or support for personal and practical difficulties such as physical or sensory impairments, medical conditions, mental health difficulties and learning difficulties. The most obvious impacts on learning to read and write are hearing impairments (especially in relation to sound/letter work in writing) and visual impairments. It is worth noting that one in three people with learning difficulties also have a sensory impairment.

It is a good idea to seek specialist help and advice if you feel that you are not able to support a particular learner adequately. The Access For All guidance document provides a first port of call:

> Access For All is the DfES guidance manual on making the adult literacy and numeracy core curricula accessible to all learners. It details the different ways in which learning needs can impact upon a learner's literacy skills. It also outlines a number of useful techniques that tutors can follow to ensure that they fully support the learning of all learners. It is available free from the DfES (see References section at end of this Lifeline).

Although smaller organisations may have experience and built-up expertise, resources and additional support may be an issue. Try to work with the special needs staff in your LEA's school support services or in your local FE college. There may even be training opportunities that you can access.

Dyslexia

Dyslexia is commonly described as 'a difficulty with processing written language'. However, there are many definitions of dyslexia but no clear consensus. There is considerable debate around whether it can be 'distinguished in practice from other possible causes of adults' literacy difficulties.' (*NRDC Research Review* 17)

Dyslexia tendencies can manifest themselves in different ways in the classroom. If you suspect that a learner may be dyslexic it is important to seek specialist advice and/or support. The following may alert you to a possible difficulty:

- A persistent or severe problem with spelling easy or common words, even after practice.
- A big difference between confidence and ability to express oneself in spoken and written language.
- Difficulties remembering the image of a word, what it looks like.
- Transposing letter such as 'd' and 'b'.
- Very slow reading speed.
- Problems following and understanding text: forgetting what has just been read, losing place in the text, having to read sentences and paragraphs over and over again.
- Needing to concentrate on forming the letters, forgetting what was going to be written, writing very slowly, producing very little text.
- Difficulties remembering information such as instructions especially when given verbally.
- Problems organising information.
- Difficulties remembering how to sequence information, e.g. the alphabet, months of the year or telephone numbers.

The Dyslexia Handbook
Tower Hamlets College in East London have produced a guide for students that explains some of the theories and misunderstandings about dyslexia in straightforward language. It describes what steps a learner can take if they think they might be dyslexic and what a dyslexia assessment consists of. It also names lots of famous people who are dyslexic and two students talk about the positive benefits of being assessed.

- Handwriting may be untidy and irregular. It may get worse when the learner is under pressure or someone is watching. It may also change quite markedly from one day to the next. There can be a lack of fluency in expressing ideas and difficulties with pronouncing and recognising words, even when they are familiar to the leaner.
- A poor sense of time.
- A poor sense of direction.
- Weak eye/hand co-ordination.
- Visual difficulties – text may 'dance' – get bigger or smaller or disappear altogether towards the margins.

Supporting dyslexic learners

Access for All (DfES, 2002) and *A framework for understanding dyslexia* (DfES, 2004) identify, describe and illustrate the current theories of dyslexia, and examine the various teaching and learning approaches used with adult dyslexic learners in literacy, language and numeracy. (See References section for texts on dyslexia.)

12 Training to become a literacy teacher, supporter or volunteer

New compulsory qualifications for people who would like to teach essential literacy and numeracy to adults in England were introduced in 2002. If you want to teach basic skills it is important to be properly qualified!

It needs to be acknowledged that opportunities for training are uneven across the country. Some regions have specialist Skills for Life Professional Development Centres (PDCs) with a range of courses and different models of training available, others may only be able to offer a very limited choice.

There is a nationwide shortage of teacher trainers who are qualified to deliver specialist literacy teacher training courses. This in turn means that the rate at which tutors are gaining access to appropriate qualifications is not as fast as it could be. The problem is even more acute in numeracy. However, the picture is constantly changing and new models of delivery of teacher training are in the process of development.

The demand on providers to put in place whole organisation strategic plans around Skills for Life has led to greater job and career opportunities for literacy and numeracy tutors. Many FE colleges for example are now employing full-time and fractional staff in literacy, numeracy and ESOL rather than relying entirely on staff on part-time contracts. There is a national shortage of specialist LLN teachers, career prospects are improving and those teachers with recognised qualifications will be in demand!

More information about teacher training for basic skills tutors can be found from the following organisations:

- **The Department for Education and Skills** also has information on training requirements: www.dfes.gov.uk/readwriteplus/Information_on_Teacher_Training On this site you can also find a list of Higher Education establishments that offer courses for becoming fully qualified basic skills teachers (though the FENTO list is more comprehensive) and a regularly updated bulletin on the latest changes.
- **The Basic Skills Agency** can advise you on where to go next, or how to find a course. Part of their website is dedicated to helping answer your questions about training – go to www.basic-skills.co.uk and do a search for 'teacher training' in the search box.

- **talent** (training adult literacy, ESOL and numeracy tutors) is the London online community of adult basic skills teaching. It carries information for people who want to become adult literacy, ESOL and numeracy teachers, materials for teachers and teacher trainers, news items and a noticeboard for views and comments. Useful for those outside London as well. www.talent.ac.uk
- **The North West Skills for Life Professional Development Project** has produced guidance for tutors involved in recruiting to Level 4 programmes in Literacy and Numeracy and a chart detailing progression options to qualified status. www.nwpdp.org

An OCN award is available at three levels for workers who will come across adults with basic skills needs in the course of their work. It was originally developed by the University of Sussex, Centre for Continuing Education, Hollington Horizons (a community outreach project managed by them and funded through ESF), the LEA and the WEA who now roll it out in Sussex. The course covers a range of areas that volunteers or other workers may experience during their work including Equal Opportunities, Data Protection, confidentiality, and Basic Skills awareness and signposting. The project was originally funded by NIACE through the Adult and Community Learning Fund.

13 Check it out

- Adult literacy learners bring with them a wealth of life experience. Use these experiences on which to base your work together.
- Devise or find assessment procedures which suit your learners and which meet the requirements of the Common Inspection Framework.
- Carry out initial and diagnostic assessment activities with your learners and use the results to plan learning and set goals and targets.
- Draw up Individual Learning Plans which are real working documents and understandable and useful for learners.
- Plan learning using the Core Curriculum as a framework, but devise activities and tasks that suit your context for working, are relevant to the lives of the learners and are interesting and fun.
- Develop formative assessment practices that involve learners in monitoring their own and others' progress.
- Celebrate achievement – whether or not it results in a formally recognised qualification.
- Make links with other providers and ensure learners have the advice, information and support they need to progress to further learning opportunities.
- Access professional development opportunities for all staff.
- Use Access for All to support learners with specific learning needs and seek specialist help where necessary.
- Keep up to date with developments and debates in the adult literacy world.
- Share materials, ideas, experiences and good practice – enjoy what you are doing and your learners will too!

Useful glossaries of *Skills for Life* terminology
- The Literacy, ESOL and Numeracy Core Curriculum Documents, *Access for All* and the *Subject Specifications for Teachers* include glossaries of terms used in subject theory and practice.
- The Workplace Basic Skills Network has a very clear and concise glossary of terms and acronyms. Go to: www.lancs.ac.uk/wbsnet/providertoolkit/glossary.htm

Tutor resources and teaching materials

Stockists and agencies

Avanti Books *Definitive stockists of teaching materials, reading books, dictionaries and journals for adult literacy learners and tutors. Lots of adult learners' own writing.*
Unit 8 Parsons Green, Stevenage, Herts SG1 4QG. Tel: 00438 350155

Brown and Brown *Produce photocopiable booklets and workpacks for adult literacy learners. Also available through Avanti (above).*
Keeper's Cottage ,Westward, Wigton,Cumbria,CA7 8NQ. Tel/fax: 01697 342915

DfES *Essential reference texts, Core Curricula, policy documents and teaching resources, many free, some downloadable from their website. Titles also cover Learning difficulties and disabilities, workplace and family learning, work with refugees and asylum seekers and embedded literacy, numeracy and ESOL.*
For a complete list, go to www.dfes.gov.uk/readwriteplus. Order from prolog: dfes@prolog.uk.com or tel: 0845 602 2260

Basic Skills Agency *Range of publications, including diagnostic packs, policy discussion papers, teaching resource packs, readers. Many documents on-line.*
The Basic Skills Agency, Commonwealth House, 1-19 New Oxford Street, London WC1A 1NU. Tel: 020 7405 4017. Email: enquiries@basic-skills.co.uk or visit www.basic-skills.co.uk

National Literacy Trust *Excellent online learning information resource. Comprehensive information on all aspects of Skills for Life policy and provision, links to other sites, recommended resources and thought-provoking policy discussion papers, e.g. on social inclusion. Visit www.literacytrust.org.uk*

Research

National Research and Development Centre for Adult Literacy and Numeracy (NRDC) *Useful reports of research and literature reviews, eg Teaching and Learning Writing, a review of research and practice; Adult Literacy Learners' difficulties in reading, an exploratory study; ICT and adult literacy, numeracy and ESOL. Also produce a free journal for practitioners: Reflect, the magazine of NRDC.*
Institute of Education, University of London, 20 Bedford Way, London WC1H 0AL, Tel: 020 7612 6476 Fax: 020 7612 6671 Email: info@nrdc.org.uk or visit www.nrdc.org.uk

Journals

*   **Adults Learning** by *NIACE is the only monthly magazine dedicated to all aspects of adult education and learning in the UK. Published 10 times a year, it is essential reading for practitioners and policy makers, offering an informed mix of news, analysis, expert commentary and feature writing.*
    Visit www.niace.org.uk to subscribe
*   **Basic Skills Bulletin** *Independent monthly magazine on Basic Skills issues.*
    Simon Boyd publishing Ltd, 34 Kimberley Rd, Cambridge CB4 1HH. Tel: 01223 513551. Email: sboydpublishing@aol.com
*   **Research and Practice in Adult Literacy Journal (RaPAL)** *Independent journal publishing articles on practitioner-based research in adult literacy work three times a year.*
    www.literacy.lancs.ac.uk/rapal Membership: w.moss@citylit.ac.uk
*   **Reflect** *NRDC, free magazine for practitioners, policy-makers and researchers.*
    Tel: 020 7612 6476 or e-mail: info@nrdc.org.uk
*   **Basic Skills** *For all teachers of literacy and numeracy in schools and post-compulsory education. Published termly.*
    All articles and reviews can be viewed online at www.basic-skills.co.uk
*   **Update** *Free DfES Newsletter for everyone providing literacy and numeracy opportunities to adults*

Accreditation and tests

*   Literacy and numeracy sample test papers can be downloaded from the QCA website: www.qca.org.uk
*   For information about recognised qualifications for adult literacy, go to the DfES website: www.dfes.gov.uk/readwriteplus

Online teaching resources

*   **www.bbc.co.uk/skillswise**
    BBC site for *Skills for Life* teaching resources. Largely L1 resources with lesson plans. Factsheets, worksheets mapped to core curricula, quizzes and games,

news stories and learners' writing. There is a free booklet available to accompany the site available from: Skillswise, PO Box 7000, Manchester, M60 3HE.

- **www.members.aol.com/skillsworkshop**
  Abingdon and Witney College site, providing range of activities, free worksheets (many mapped to Adult Literacy Core Curriculum), lesson plans and links to other recommended sites.
- **http://www.usingenglish.com/links/**
  Tests, quizzes, printable materials and articles, mainly for ESL learners.
- **http://www.spelling.hemscott.net/**
  US Website for Spelling it Right – aimed at adults who want to improve their spelling as well as children. Downloadable worksheets.

Useful contacts and networks

Adult Learning Inspectorate (ALI)
Website: www.ali.gov.uk
ALI has a Good Practice Database
containing detailed case studies of
good practice highlighted in
inspections: click on the Excalibur tab
on the main ALI website.

Basic Skills Agency (BSA)
Commonwealth House
1-19 New Oxford Street
London WC1A 1NU
Tel: 0207 4054017
Website: www.basic-skills.co.uk

Campaign for Learning
19 Buckingham St.
London WC2N 6EF
Tel: 020 7930 1111
Fax: 020 7930 1551
Email: campaign@campaign-for-
learning.org.uk

**Learning Skills Development Agency
(LSDA)**
LSDA Head Office
Learning & Skills Development Agency
Regent Arcade House,
19-25 Argyll Street,
London W1F 7LS
Switchboard: 020 7297 9000
Fax: 020 7297 9001
For further information about LSDA or
any of its activities contact the
Information Services team.
Tel: 020 7297 9144
Fax: 020 7297 9242
Email: enquiries@LSDA.org.uk

LearnDirect – a Government initiative to
promote online learning.
To enquire about **learndirect** courses
call the helpline on 0800 101 901
or visit the website:
www.learndirect.co.uk

Learning and Skills Council (LSC)
Website: www.lsc.gov.uk
Responsible for funding post-16
education and training in England. This
is the national office address. There are
47 local councils throughout the
country. The regional office addresses
can be found on the LSC website.

London Language and Literacy Unit (LLU+)
Website: http://www.sbu.ac.uk/lllu/

National Literacy Trust
Website: www.literacytrust.org.uk

National Research and Development Centre for Adult Literacy and Numeracy (NRDC)
Website: www.nrdc.org.uk

Qualifications and Curriculum Authority (QCA)
Website: www.qca.org.uk
QCA have approved literacy and numeracy qualifications and they are available now. Information can be found on their website

RAPAL
Research and Practice in Adult Literacy Group
Website: www.literacy.lancs.ac.uk/rapal

Workplace Basic Skills Network
CSET
Website: www.lancs.ac.uk/wbsnet

Other useful websites

dfes@prolog.uk.com – All of the documents relating to the Skills for Life national strategy, a range of teaching and assessment materials as well as a quarterly newsletter can be ordered free from the dfes at this site.

learn.co.uk – Guardian resource for school teachers that has interesting lesson plans that could be adapted

lifelonglearning.co.uk – Links to key sites

Ofsted.gov.uk – college inspection reports

qca.org.uk – new basic skills qualifications for learners

skillbuild.co.uk – Axis education – downloadable materials for literacy and numeracy, information about further publications

standards.dfes.gov.uk – the national curriculum site for schools, useful for family literacy and numeracy

writeonline.co.uk – interactive story writing software for teaching creative writing and composition

Useful international websites

Educational Resources Information Center (US) –
www.eric.ed.gov

Languages Australia – the National Languages & Literacy Institute of Australia –
http://languageaustralia.com.au

National Adult Literacy Database (Canada) –
http://www.nald.ca/

National Center for the Study of Adult Learning and Literacy (US) –
http://gseweb.harvard.edu/~ncsall/

National Institute for Literacy (US) –
http://novel.nifl.gov